Indians of the Andes

The Indians of the Andes Mountains in South America are a people without a history. Their origin is shrouded in legend, but most archaeologists agree that they are descendants of people who migrated across the Bering Strait from Mongolia thousands of years ago. The Indians suffered little hardship under the rule of the Incas, but were treated badly by the Spaniards who conquered the Inca Empire in the sixteenth century. They took away the Indians' lands and forced them into slavery. Little changed until the 1950s, when people began to take note of the Indians' desperate plight. Since then there have been land reforms and improved medical and educational facilities. But it remains to be seen whether these will encourage the Indians to remain on their lands or whether they will continue to move to the towns, hoping for an easier and more affluent life. Marion Morrison has spent the last twenty years traveling throughout South America while researching and writing. During this period she spent several years working among the Aymara Indians in Bolivia.

Original Peoples

INDIANS
OF THE ANDES

Marion Morrison

Rourke Publications, Inc.
Vero Beach, FL 32964

Original Peoples

Eskimos — The Inuit of the Arctic
Aborigines of Australia
Plains Indians of North America
South Pacific Islanders
Indians of the Andes
Zulus of Southern Africa

Frontispiece *Fiesta-time for some
Aymara Indians from Lake Titicaca.*

First published in the
United States in 1987 by
Rourke Publications, Inc.
Vero Beach, FL 32964

Library of Congress Cataloging-in-Publication Data

Morrison, Marion.
  Indians of the Andes.

  (Original peoples)
  Bibliography: p.
  Includes index.
  Summary: Introduces the history, culture, and daily life of the Indians who
live in the highlands of South America's Andes Mountains.
  1. Indians of South America — Andes Region — Juvenile literature.
[1. Indians of South America — Andes Region. 2. Andes Region] I. Title. II.
Series.
F2229.M86 1987 980'.004'98 87-4334
ISBN 0-086625-260-6

Photoset by Direct Image Photosetting
Printed in Italy 'by G. Canale & C.S.p.A., Turin

Contents

Introduction   6

Chapter 1 In the Beginning
Aymara and Quechua   8
Uru-Chipaya: People of the Tombs   10

Chapter 2 Rise and Fall of the Incas
The Incas   12
Monuments and a Lost City   14
Lust for Gold and Silver   16
Revolt and War   18

Chapter 3 Daily Life
Pachamama and Other Gods   20
Land above the Clouds   23
Beasts of Burden   24
Aymara and Quechua Dress   26

Chapter 4 Revolution and Change
Coming of the Campesino   28
Back to the Land   30
The Need for Education   32
Witch Doctors and Medicine   34

Chapter 5 Today and Tomorrow
Coca: Green Gold of the Andes   36
Colonization of the Lowlands   38
The Otavalo Indians of Ecuador   40
The Mestizos   42
The Future   44

Glossary   46
Books to Read   46
Glossary of Indian and Spanish Words   47
Index   48

Introduction

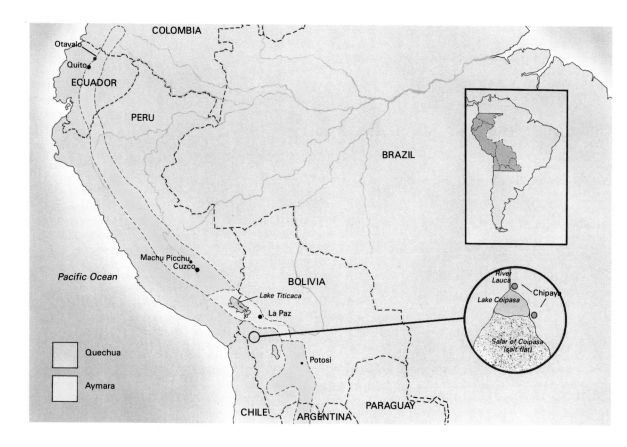

The Andes mountains of South America extend from the Caribbean shores of Colombia in the north, to Cape Horn at the southern tip of the continent. Many of the highest peaks reach to over 20,000 feet, (608 meters) and where the range breaks into smaller branches, or *cordilleras,* there are deep, green valleys and flat, bleak plains. Most of these valleys and plains are over 12,000 feet (365 meters) above sea level, and are the home of the Andean Indians. The largest group of Indians are the

This map shows the locations of the groups of Indians discussed in this book.

Quechua. Most of them live in Peru, Bolivia and Ecuador, but some also inhabit Colombia and Argentina. And the second largest group, the Aymara, have their homes around the shores of Lake Titicaca, the highest navigable lake in the world, on the border of Peru and Bolivia.

In the fifteenth century, this land was ruled by the Incas. The Incas were famous for their agriculture

6

and engineering achievements.

In 1532, Pizarro, the Spanish general, landed on the coast of Peru, marched his soldiers over some of the highest Andes and conquered the Incas. The Andean Indians suffered badly under the Spanish. Their land was taken away and they were forced into slavery on farms and in mines. During the 400 years after the conquest, the Indian way of life changed very little, even though the countries of South America broke away from Spain to become independent in the nineteenth century.

The Indians waited until the twentieth century for any notice to be taken of their desperate situation. In the last thirty years the Andean governments have introduced laws giving the Indians education and returning their land. This is a story of a people who have managed to survive despite hardship and oppression, and who, only now, are beginning to enter the modern world.

An Indian village high up in the Andes Mountains of eastern Peru.

Chapter 1 **In the Beginning**

Aymara and Quechua

The Indians of the Andes are a people without a history. Their origin is hidden in legend. The Quechua tell of white, bearded men who came to their land, taught men to sow seeds and harvest corn, and who then sailed away to the west. The Aymara believe their god Viracocha rose from the cold waters of Lake Titicaca to create a world of darkness and giants. When the giants angered him, he turned them to stone. Then he created a new world with sun, moon, stars and people of normal size.

Archaeologists, too, are not certain of the origins of the Andean people. But most agree that the early peoples migrated from Mongolia across the Bering Strait (between Alaska and the U.S.S.R.), and made their way south into the temperate lands of the Andes. These early people were hunters, who later turned to simple farming.

Close by Lake Titicaca, on the largest of the high plains, the *altiplano,* are the ruins of Tiwanaku. Tiwanaku is also a mystery. Seen today it is a mass of huge stone blocks, or megaliths, which may have been a temple or a ceremonial center. There are stone figures of men and some carvings. Most famous is the Gateway of the Sun, a single block weighing over 10 tons. The Aymara believe these megaliths are the giants turned into stone by Viracocha. But to archaeologists, the mystery is who built Tiwanaku and how were such huge stones erected. What is certain is that it needed a well-organized society of many thousands of people, and from what we know of the Aymara today, it seems unlikely to have been any of their ancestors.

This impressive stone figure can be found in the ruins at Tiwanaku.

Quechua Indians buying and selling produce at a market in a Peruvian village.

Uru-Chipaya: People of the Tombs

Just one small group of the early hunting tribes, known as the Uru-Chipaya, survives today and lives on a remote Andean salt marsh in western Bolivia. The Chipayas, as they are called, say they are the oldest people in the world, and that they are "the people of the tombs." Their tombs, or *chullpas,* stand above the ground. In the tombs there are mummies covered by the same cloth as the Chipayas use today.

The men dress in dull-brown sleeveless tunics, made from hand-spun llama and sheep wool, worn over trousers of loosely spun wool, with a narrow belt or sling on which they hang their keys and other small possessions. Chipaya women wear a simple tunic woven from llama wool and spend many hours braiding their hair into one hundred tiny braids. It is an ancient hairstyle and still found, tied in this way, on skulls in the tombs.

Chipaya houses are unlike any of the huts of the other Andean peoples. They are round and built

Chipaya women wear their hair in braids. The Chipayas live on a salt marsh in western Bolivia (see the map on page 6).

from sods of cut turf; their domed roofs are thatched with a tough grass, called *ichu*. Each house has only one opening, on the side away from the prevailing wind, and as there is no wood, the Chipayas use dried cactus for the door and for roof supports.

Hunting has been the Indians' traditional way of life, and in the salt marshes they catch ducks, geese and flamingos. This is done with a *bolas*, a Y-shaped cord with stones at the three ends. The *bolas* is thrown

A Chipaya village with its distinctive huts thatched with grass.

so that it winds itself around the legs of a flying bird and brings it down.

The last Uru Indian died twenty years ago, but the traditions of his people have survived. Today on Lake Titicaca, Aymara Indians live on the floating "Uru" islands and fish with boats made from the totora reed that grows along the shores of the lake, in much the same way as the Urus did for 2,000 years.

11

Chapter 2 **Rise and Fall of the Incas**

The Incas

In A.D. 1200 the Inca people were one of many tribes living in the Peruvian Andes. Their power developed gradually until 1438, when Pachacuti Inca became Emperor. Pachacuti and his son Topa Inca were brilliant

By the 1500s, the Inca Empire stretched down most of the west coast of South America.

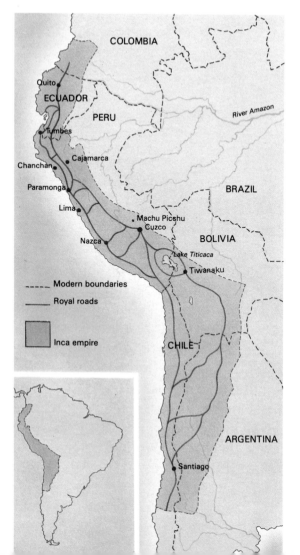

generals, and by the time Topa Inca died in 1493, the Inca Empire extended from Ecuador to Chile.

Although the Empire covered a vast, difficult terrain, it was simply and strictly run. It was divided into four great provinces with Cuzco, the capital, at the center. From Cuzco, excellent roads were constructed to every part of the Empire, across the mountains to the Amazon jungles in the east and Pacific coast in the west. Resthouses, called *tambos*, were placed along the roads, sometimes with special storehouses to feed 25,000 men, because the Emperor always traveled in great style and with many thousands of helpers.

The Emperor was believed to be descended from the Sun God, and his Queen came from his own family, although he was allowed any number of secondary wives. Noblemen, mostly from the Emperor's family, governed the four provinces, together with administrators, army officers and priests, all of whom had special privileges. The ordinary people in villages and cities lived in *ayllus,* or communities, which were either family groups or groups formed for administrative purposes.

Inca society had a place for everyone and work for them to do. All the land that could be cultivated was divided into three parts and farmed by the peasants. The first part, for the gods, provided food for the priests and offerings for sacrifices. The second part produced crops, not only for the Emperor and his noblemen, but also for the sick and the needy. And the third part was for the peasants.

Very few people suffered real hardship under Inca rule, although law and order were very strict and several crimes were punishable by death.

The Inca fortress of Sacsahuaman. In the background is Cuzco, which was the capital of the Inca Empire.

Monuments and a Lost City

The Incas were also remarkable for the fact that they had no written language. Instead they used an accounting device known as a *quipu*. The *quipu* was a long peice of string to which a number of other colored pieces were attached, and these had knots tied in them. The colors represented information and the knots showed numbers. It was a complicated system and understood only by special keepers, who were called *quipumayocs*.

A quipu *was used for recording numbers and other information.*

Although the Incas were skilled weavers and potters, their greatest monuments are their buildings. Without knowledge of the wheel, and using only simple tools of wood, stone and bronze, craftsmen carved enormous blocks of stone that were positioned into walls and buildings by using ropes, sleds and earthen ramps. So finely were the blocks carved that no mortar was needed to fill the gaps.

Temples were built in every town, many of them elaborately decorated with ornaments of copper, silver and gold.

Rumors of the Incas' wealth began to reach Europe soon after Columbus discovered the Americas in 1492. In 1532, the Spaniard Francisco Pizarro landed on the coast of Peru with only 180 men. The Incas were just recovering from a terrible civil war in which Atahualpa had killed his brother and made himself Emperor. Atahualpa was imprisoned by the Spaniards, who demanded a huge ransom of gold for his release. A fortune was gathered from every part of the Emperor, but nonetheless Atahualpa was executed.

With the fall of the Inca Empire, many people sought refuge in the nearby mountains. One of the last towns occupied by the Inca people was Machu Picchu, sometimes called the Lost City of the Incas. Hidden for many years in thick forest, it was rediscovered in 1911 and is now visited by thousands of tourists.

The ruins of Machu Picchu, one of the last strongholds of the Incas, high in the Andes Mountains. Hidden for many years, this "Lost City" was rediscovered in 1911.

Lust for Gold and Silver

The Spanish *conquistadores* arrived in South America with two ambitions: to search for gold and precious minerals, and to convert the local people to Christianity.

One of the most savage excesses of the Spanish was their abuse of the *mita*, an Inca system of compulsory work. The Spanish used the *mita* to force the Indians to work in the mines. Whole families were compelled to travel with their animals over hundreds of miles, leaving behind them entire regions uninhabited, to work in places like Potosi in south Bolivia, famous for its silver mine, the Cerro Rico.

At any one time, 14 percent of all men were on the *mita,* which lasted for four months each year. Men spent up to thirty-six hours continuously underground, and many thousands died in the mines. The Indians earned little money, and after paying compulsory taxes, they often found themselves in debt. These debts were in turn inherited by children and grandchildren, who could only repay them by a lifetime's work in the mines.

When they were not working in the mines, the Indians were forced into agricultural service for the Spaniards who had taken over their lands. By a system known as *encomienda,* the new landlords could acquire an Indian work force in return for instructing them in the Christian faith. Such instruction was often little more than a ritual baptism, while the Indians were committed to a life of perpetual slavery.

To add to their miserable existence, the Indians were also exposed to many new diseases brought in by the colonists from Europe. So disastrous were the combined effects of illness and maltreatment, that the Indian population declined catastrophically. Some estimates say that more than 90 percent of the Indian people disappeared in the first one hundred years after the Spanish conquest.

The gold-plated altar of the church of La Compania in Quito, Ecuador.

The Virgin of Guadelupe in Sucre Cathedral, Bolivia. Made of gold and silver and studded with many precious stones, she is an appropriate symbol of the wealth that attracted Spaniards to South America.

Revolt and War

San Antonio de Lipez, an old Spanish mining town. It was deserted after the Indian risings in the late eighteenth century.

The years following the Spanish conquest until independence were a time of insurrection and revolt among the Andean peoples. There were a number of different reasons for this.

The population was very mixed. The conquering Spaniards were mostly adventurers who had not brought wives or families with them. They intermarried with the local population, creating a new race of "mestizos." At times there were revolts between mestizos and the Spanish. Other clashes occurred between *peninsulares* (Spaniards born in Spain who had emigrated to South America) and *criollos* (pure-blooded Spaniards born in South America). Then there were Indian insurrections.

An epidemic occurred in 1719 that reduced the population of Potosi from something over 160,000 to 60,000. This, together with much

18

discontent and resentment over the barbarous conditions of work to which the Indians were subjected, led to a rebellion in 1780 which spread throughout Peru and Bolivia. Quechuas and Aymaras joined forces, and in 1780 the city of La Paz, today the capital of Bolivia, was besieged by 80,000 Indians. The siege lasted almost nine months, until the Indians were defeated and the leaders of the rebellion executed. In Ecuador, too, there were major Indian uprisings from 1770 to the end of the century.

The next revolt was of a different kind. This time the Spanish colonists turned against the Spanish Crown and the Indians were not involved. The fight for independence was taken up all over South America, led by Simón Bolívar in the north and José de San Martin in the south. In 1821 the Republic of Peru was created, that of Bolivia in 1825 and of Ecuador in 1830.

However the status of the Indian remained unchanged. The Church, which had become the biggest land-owner and very wealthy, did little to help them.

Some old Spanish coins, which were minted in Potosi, southern Bolivia.

Chapter 3 **Daily Life**

Pachamama and Other Gods

Aymara and Quechua Indians have always had their own form of worship. Theirs is a simple religion and relates to things around them that they consider most important. The word *huaca* is something holy or magical, and the Indians revere *huacas* in the form of mountains, rivers, lakes, caves and even stones.

Since the time of the Incas, the Aymara and Quechua Indians have honored gods and goddesses with festivals at significant times in the agricultural year. The first festival of the year in Inca times was devoted to Illapu or Thuñupa, the Storm God, because the small seeds needed steady rain to help them grow. August, the month of plowing, was the festival of Pachamama, Mother Earth, and the most important celebration, the Inti Raimi, or Sun Festival, followed the harvest in June.

The Spanish priests soon realized that Christianity could only be introduced if the Indians were allowed to keep their ancient traditions. And so the two religions developed together. Some of the many Spanish churches, cathedrals and monasteries were built on the foundations of Inca temples. Most significantly in Cuzco, the Church of Santo Domingo was constructed on top of the Sun Temple, the Incas' most revered shrine.

Indian festivals and ceremonies were also made to coincide with important dates in the Catholic calendar. Inti Raimi now occurs at the same time as the Catholic celebration of Corpus Christi. The Aymaras and Quechuas adjusted easily to the splendid rituals, and

Celebrating Corpus Christi, which coincides with Inti Raimi.

An Aymara Indian at a Morenada dance in Bolivia.

with much singing and dancing they take part in the pageants and processions, helping to parade saintly figures around the towns. But their hearts and minds remain firmly with their own gods, particularly Pachamama, and the spirits of the natural world around them.

21

Quechua Indians harvesting in Cuzco Valley, Peru. With little water, hard and barren soil, and wide variations in daytime and nighttime temperatures, farming has never been easy for the Indians.

Land above the Clouds

In the communities, or *ayllus,* of the mountain valleys and plains where the Indians live, harvesting the land has never been easy. There is little water; the soil is hard and barren; and because of the altitude, the sun is strong and hot during the day, and the temperature well below freezing at night. The irrigation techniques and agricultural terraces developed by the Incas ensured adequate food

A drawing, depicting farming in Inca times, by the chronicler Guaman Poma, who kept a record of Inca life.

throughout the Empire, but these systems were neglected by the Spanish. Today the Indians cultivate only a small percentage of the land once worked by the Incas.

Yet for centuries the Indians have produced a variety of crops. Some, like the potato and beans, are known to us; others, like *quinoa,* a nutritious cereal, are native to the Andes.

Farming tools used by the men have changed little over the centuries. Digging sticks with iron tips and clod-breakers are still used, although since the days of the Spanish, the primitive plow drawn by a yoke of oxen can be seen in many parts of the mountains.

Around the shores of Lake Titicaca, where there is an abundant supply of water, the fields are always colorful with plants and vegetables. Pigs, sheep and cows graze among the totora reed and on nearby grass, and the Aymara Indians supplement their diet with fish from the lake. The Indians eat little meat, though on fiesta days they enjoy guinea pig, which they raise in their homes, or chicken.

All the Indians chew coca, a leaf which they believe has magical properties. Coca grows in the warm lowland valleys on the eastern side of the mountains. Chewing the leaf helps to numb the constant pangs of hunger and cold experienced by the Indians in their high, hostile homeland.

Beasts of Burden

The Indians still live in mud houses similar to those of the workers in Inca times. The one-room dwellings are made from adobe brick and have roofs thatched with grass or reeds. Usually there are no windows and the one door normally faces east. Inside there is little furniture and the family sleep on adobe mud platforms covered with llama pelts. Just a few cooking utensils and pots are kept in niches in the walls.

As the sun rises in the morning, the Indian emerges from his home and makes his way along stony roads and tracks, herding his llamas and sheep to grazing land. The llama, together with its close relatives, the alpaca, vicuna and guanaco, belongs to the camel family, but it has no hump. The vicuna and guanaco are wild, and the fur of the vicuna has always been prized as it is very fine and soft. At the time of the Incas, only the Emperor and his noblemen were allowed to wear the fur, and the penalty for killing vicuna was death.

Strong, surefooted and capable of carrying a heavy load, the llama is very important to the Andean Indian.

24

The Indians domesticated llamas as long ago as 500 B.C., and the beast is as important to the mountain people now as it was then. The women spin and weave the wool into clothes and blankets: llama dung can be used as fertilizer and is regularly used as fuel for fires. A llama fetus is often buried in the foundations of a new house to bring good fortune. At fiesta time, the elegant, haughty beasts are decorated with tassels of colored wool through their ears and around their necks, and they are treated with great ceremony.

The Indians value the llama most of all as a pack animal, as it is strong, surefooted and capable of carrying a load of 50 pounds or more over long stretches of winding mountain tracks.

A drove of vicunas. Their fur has always been prized for its softness and fineness.

Below *Typical Indian houses, made of adobe blocks with thatched roofs.*

Aymara and Quechua Dress

Aymara and Quechua Indians, while similar in many ways, have retained distinctive styles of dress.

The Aymara women are the most colorful and can be recognized easily in their huge skirts, or *polleras*. *Polleras* are made of brilliantly colored heavy cotton, gathered tight at the waist and swirling out like a crinoline. A woman wears several of these skirts at the same time,

A Quechua Indian girl drinking chicha, beer made from corn.

probably her entire wardrobe, and the greater the number of skirts, the greater is her apparent wealth.

Over the *pollera* is a blouse of rough cotton, then a woolen blanket doubled over the shoulders, and finally a bright, striped cotton shawl, called an *aguayo*. In the *aguayo*, the Aymara woman carries her baby and other bundles everywhere she goes. Some of the Indian women wear bowler hats, a custom said to have been adopted about fifty years ago when British workmen arrived in Bolivia to build the railroads.

Alongside the women, the men are more conservative, wearing baggy, rough cotton trousers, covered by a long earth-colored poncho. On his feet the Indian man wears sandals made from the rubber of old tires, and on his head a *chullo,* a knitted hat.

Quechua clothing changes to some extent from one community to another, though in general the men wear short pants and open shirts, and a short poncho. The women wear just one, long skirt. The most interesting piece of the Quechua Indians' clothing, though, is the hat. Each community has its own style, anything from large, flat, black boards with tassels, to close fitting woven hats.

At fiesta time, the Indian women wear their best dresses of velvet, silk or satin, in deep rich blues and reds, with elaborate decorations, ribbons and braids.

A colorful crowd of Quechua Indians at a fiesta in Peru.

Chapter 4 **Revolution and Change**

Coming of the Campesino

At the beginning of this century, while the Andean Indians unhappily accepted their status at the poorest level of society, a few people were beginning to voice concern about their situation.

Their words might have gone unheeded had war not broken out in 1932 between Bolivia and Paraguay over a disputed area of land, called the Chaco, which borders the two countries. During the war, which lasted three years, people of all levels of society fought alongside each other, and for the first time everyone saw how badly off the Indians were. Undernourished and poorly clothed, they suffered extremely high casualties. But from this grim experience, people realized that something had to be done. And Bolivia, the country that had suffered most in the war, took the lead in introducing measures designed to improve conditions for the Aymara and Quechua Indians.

At first, the richer people opposed these measures, until in 1952 a political party came into power in Bolivia prepared to implement three important reforms. The first was to nationalize the mines. The second was to reform agriculture so that anyone over 18, who wished to farm, was entitled to own land. The third was an educational act by which all children could have schooling.

It was about this time that the word *campesino,* meaning "peasant," came into use in Bolivia. The term "Indian" was thought to be degrading and was no longer to be used. The Indians of Peru and Ecuador had to wait longer for similar reforms, but in the last few years there has been a serious attempt in all the Andean countries to provide the Indians with a better way of life.

A statue in Potosi, Bolivia, to mark the nationalization of the mines in 1952.

Below *A group of Andean miners.*

Above *Bolivian workers celebrating the 1952 revolution in La Paz, the capital.*

Back to the Land

Of all the new measures that have now been introduced, Indians everywhere have most welcomed land reforms. They had long wanted to recover the rights to their land taken from them by the Spanish. So desperate were the Indians in Bolivia that, following the Chaco War where they had the opportunity to mix with whites and mestizos, they began to take matters into their own hands. With increased confidence, they tried to lease back their lands, occasionally using force, and as a more unified and better organized group, they became a problem for the Bolivian government. So, inevitably, there was much rejoicing among the Aymaras and Quechuas when the land reform law was finally passed. The Indians celebrated for several days and nights.

With the return of their lands, however, Indians in all parts of the mountains have had to face new problems. By law, the large estates were broken up into small units, which do not produce enough to make them economical. The Indians need money for seeds and fertilizers, and the technical knowledge to

Tape recorders and radios on sale in a market in La Paz.

handle farm machinery to make the most of their small farms.

Additionally, the Aymaras and Quechuas have only recently become accustomed to using trucks and railroads to carry their produce to the towns. Previously, they were forced to carry the harvest on their backs, many hundreds of miles. Selling in the towns has in turn brought them into contact with the "cash economy" — exchanging money, not goods, for their produce. The Indians

Quechua Indians harvesting a potato crop in Peru.

are becoming members of a consumer society, using their money to buy machine-made clothes, and some small luxury items, like transistor radios.

The Indians have benefited in one very important respect from land reform: they have regained their self-respect and can now be counted as citizens within their own countries.

31

The Need for Education

In Bolivia, before 1952, only a very small percentage of the population could vote. One of the first acts of the new government was to give the right to vote to everyone over 21 years old, even if, like the Indians, they could not read or write. In Peru, men and women over 21 are eligible to vote, while in Ecuador this right is extended only to citizens over 18 who are literate.

Clearly, there is a great need to educate the Indian peoples, to teach them to read and write. In many communities, the Indians have been happy to devote their time and energy to building schools, but progress is slow. There is a shortage of money for equipment and furniture. Even so, the Indian children are eager to learn and many walk miles without breakfast to get to school.

In some remote areas, where there are no schools, Indians are being taught to read and write over the radio. This helps the women, particularly, because although the Indian father is happy that his son should be educated, he needs his wife and daughters to look after the animals. So the women are beginning to form clubs where they can follow literacy classes, and learn about health and family care. They have also developed a trade in food and woolen garments, which they sell on railroad stations to tourists.

Aymara Indians from south Peru learn to read and write with the help of programs from a "radio school."

The changing face of a Bolivian market where Indians buy their goods.

As they make more contact with the outside world, women's attitudes and habits are changing. In the traditional hut, plastic buckets, safety pins and aluminum pots are beginning to appear. Sometimes a wooden bed, table and chairs have been bought, while corrugated-iron roofs and bicycles are becoming status symbols for the more successful Indian families.

Witch Doctors and Medicine

It is in matters of health that the Indians of the Andes most greatly resist change. They have always had their own form of medicine, relying on local plants and herbs. They believe illness is caused by evil spirits, best cured by a witch doctor "reading" coca leaves to find an appropriate remedy.

One group of Indians in Bolivia, the Kallawaya, are famed as traveling herbal doctors. Their name in Aymara means "to carry medicine on the shoulder," and they travel the Andes with handwoven bags filled with dried herbs.

The herbal and medical knowledge of the Kallawaya is a well-kept secret. It is known that they have

The Apu *(headman) of the Kallawaya Indians. This group is famous for being traveling herbal doctors.*

Wild herbs, which are used as medicine, on sale in a market in Las Paz, Bolivia.

been successful in curing some illnesses that once puzzled modern doctors, such as polio and pneumonia. But equally, their skill is questioned as it is partly based on Indian superstition.

Modern doctors recognize the need to introduce the Indians to the hygienic conditions of clinics and hospitals. It has not been difficult to persuade the Indians to help build their own clinics. As they did with the schools the Indians have contributed labor and money. It is a different matter when they are asked to take pills, or have injections, and the women are very reluctant to change from giving birth in their homes. This is a serious problem as the infant mortality rate is one of the highest in the world.

It is not surprising, given the harsh working conditions of the Indians and their modest diets, that they cannot expect to live for much more than 45 years. But it is for this reason that health care must be a high priority within the changes now occurring in the Andean way of life.

Chapter 5 **Today and Tomorrow**

Coca: Green Gold of the Andes

One of the many Indian legends tells how, a long time ago, the highland people were traveling from the *altiplano* into the richly forested lowland slopes on the east side of the mountains. To make clearings, the Indians decided to burn down the trees. It is said that "the fire blazed ferociously and smoke rose so high that it polluted the ice kingdom of Khuno" — the god of snow and storm. He was so angry that he sent down thunder, lightning and hail. Later when the Indians emerged from the caves where they had taken refuge, they found a single plant had survived the storm: the bright-green coca plant. Since that day, it is said, the Indians have chewed the coca leaf to relieve them of hunger and pain.

The coca leaf is now an indispensable part of Indian life and culture. A day's work is never done without a wad of leaves kept in a special hand-woven pouch. Coca is used in medicine and in certain ceremonies to foretell the future. Sacrifices of the

Coca leaves on sale in a market in Bolivia. The coca leaf is an important part of Indian life and culture.

leaves are made to Pachamama (Mother Earth) throughout the year, and they are burned to bring good luck when a new house is built.

Recently there has been a big demand in the United States and Europe for pure cocaine derived from the coca leaf. As an illegal drug, cocaine commands high prices and dealers go to any lengths to increase the supply. And so the plantations of the Andean jungle slopes are being

The Quechua Indian on the left is carrying a wad of coca leaves.

taken over for an international market. Some local growers have benefited from soaring prices, but the Indians have suffered because they now have to pay much more for their own supply. Until they have a better way of life, it is doubtful whether the Indians could survive without the stimulus given them by the leaf.

Colonization of the Lowlands

The region where the coca leaf grows is part of a vast territory that extends from the Andean foothills of Bolivia, Peru and Ecuador east to Brazil. Very few people inhabit the area, which is potentially very rich. Densely forested, there is a great

Aymara Indians beginning a new life in the Bolivian lowlands.

variety of timber; the land is good for rice, coffee, rubber, sugar and tropical fruits; and there is pasture for breeding cattle. There are also extensive oil, gas and iron-ore deposits.

It has long been recognized that the region should be developed to provide an alternative to the harsh economic conditions in the highlands. But there are immense problems, most particularly in communications. The area is isolated by the Andean mountains, and the few roads that exist are subject to heavy rains, making their muddy surface impassable for trucks. A vast network of rivers crosses the region, but rapids make navigation very difficult. As a result there are few towns, and almost no amenities, like electricity or sanitation.

Plans for colonizing the territory have been started. But it is a considerable undertaking to uproot families and encourage them to start afresh in conditions so different from those they are used to. The soil, farming techniques and produce are all strange to people from the mountains. Tropical diseases can be frightening and the one big question is whether the Indians can cope physically with the change from the cold uplands to the tropical lowlands of constant heat and humidity.

The answer seems to be that it is possible. Despite the difficulties, some tens of thousands of highland people have made the move and settled in the lowland area.

Above *Airplanes, like this one, are helping to open up the lowlands.*

Below *A cattle ranch in the Bolivian lowlands, set up by colonists.*

The Otavalo Indians of Ecuador

The Otavalo Indians of Ecuador are a success story among Andean Indians. They are an exceptional group who have retained the customs and traditions of other Indians, while at the same time making a commercial success of their talent as weavers and salespeople. An Otavalo Indian can always be recognized by his distinctive long dark-blue poncho, worn over white trousers, his wide-brimmed felt hat and single braid that reaches half way down his back.

In their homeland, a valley in the shadow of an extinct volcano, some Otavalos are farmers. These are the relatively poorer families and the cloth they weave is just for family use. The more prosperous families weave to sell, not just in markets in Ecuador, but in many other South American countries, and sometimes in Mexico and the United States.

Entire families are involved in the weaving business. On Saturdays, everyone takes off for the now famous Otavalo market. There are food and animal sections in the market, but it is the textile area that draws the dealers and tourists. Brightly colored ponchos, blankets, shawls, and woolen goods are on display, together with belts, mats, ropes and straw hats.

Since the 1950s, new machinery and developments in textiles have

An Otavalo mother and child.

Otavalo Indians at a market in Ecuador.

enabled a few Otavalos to create much bigger businesses. Newly acquired automatic looms have taken their place alongside old-fashioned wooden upright looms, and hand-powered knitting machines have been imported from Europe. Synthetic fibers, like Orlon, save the weavers a great deal of time pre- viously spent in washing, dyeing and spinning. Now, at least one success- ful Otavalo employs around one hundred workers, both Indians and whites, in the largest Indian-owned business in Ecuador.

The Mestizos

Indian houses on the outskirts of the city of La Paz, capital of Bolivia.

The "mestizo" group, created when the Spanish conquerors married into the local population, has grown in strength and numbers over the last four centuries, particularly in Peru and Bolivia. Being part-Spanish, part-Indian and speaking the language of both, they have come to play the middle role in the Andean countries. Mestizos run small businesses and shops, or work as miners, clerks, traders and domestic servants. In La Paz, Bolivia's capital, they are known as *cholos*. The women *cholas*, dressed in bowler hats and *pollera* skirts, line the sidewalks selling their wares, and are reputedly some of the wealthiest people in the city.

It is estimated that in Bolivia the population is 65 percent Indian and 30 percent mestizos. In Peru the ratio is 50 percent Indian to 35 percent mestizos. The remaining people are pure white Spanish descendants. The number of mestizos is constantly increasing as

42

the Indians leave their country homes to seek a better way of life in the towns, where they intermarry.

The towns have developed dramatically, but few Indians improve their standard of living. Entering a strange world, the Indians first need to find somewhere to live. Slums (called *barriadas*) have developed around the edges of the towns to meet the demand for homes. Families crowd into dwellings made of cardboard and corrugated iron, in which often there is no light, heat or sanitation.

The conditions are appalling, but it is from this background that a few enterprising Indians can make their way into the mestizo world.

Significantly, the truly successful mestizo rejects his Indian background completely, and if this trend continues, as seems likely, it is inevitable that in the future, the pure Indian will no longer exist.

Some cholas *parading on behalf of their street-trading unions.*

The Future

The achievements of the Incas demonstrated what could be accomplished in a well-organized society, despite the hostile environment in which they lived. And how quickly and easily all this fell into neglect after the Spanish conquest. Yet despite four hundred years of a punishing existence, the Andean Indians have survived, retaining intact many of their customs and traditions.

The future for the Indians has to be seen in the context of the countries where they live. Since independence, these countries have experienced years of upheaval in their search for political and economic stability. The Andean countries are known to have valuable resources, not only in minerals and metals from the highlands, but in agricultural produce and timber from the eastern lowlands. Both money and technical expertise is essential to develop these resources, and to tackle the immense problem of communication. The

Trucks crossing the Bolivian altiplano *at an altitude of 13,500 feet (4,100 meters).*

An Aymara Indian on his "new" tractor on the Bolivian altiplano.

mountains, while being a spectacular landscape of snowcapped peaks, create a formidable barrier to the vast expanses of jungle forest. Only when this barrier has been overcome will the Andean countries be able to unify both their land and people.

No longer, though, is it possible for anyone to ignore the place of the Indian in society. If the Andean republics are to succeed, then the Indian must play his part. With better opportunities in education, improved medical facilities and a familiarity with modern-day technology, the Indian people stand a better chance. The last thirty years have seen many changes and the Indians have found a new dignity in the repossession of their land. It remains to be seen whether they will stay on their land, or whether more and more Indians will move into towns, joining the mestizos.

Glossary

Adobe Bricks made of mud and straw and dried in the sun.

Alpaca Domesticated animal of the central Andes, related to the camel and kept for its wool.

Bolas Weapon of three weighted strings used for catching animals.

Clod-breakers Primitive implement used to break up the soil.

Domesticate To tame an animal that is used to living in the wilds.

Fertilizer A substance that is added to soil to replace lost minerals.

Fetus Unborn animal.

Guanaco Wild relative of the llama.

Independence In South America, this was the moment when each country was released from its ties with Spain.

Literacy The ability to read and write.

Llama Beast of burden, related to the camel, and native to the Andes.

Megalith Large stone monument.

Mortar A mixture of lime, sand and water used in building to hold bricks or blocks together.

Nationalize To make something the property of a nation, for example, the tin mining industry.

Pelt The cured skin of an animal.

Poncho A long piece of cloth with a slit in the middle for the head, worn like a cloak and often handwoven.

Superstition Belief in the supernatural, fear of the mysterious.

Totora A reed that grows on the shores of Lake Titicaca.

Books to Read

Some of the books listed here may no longer be in print but should still be available in libraries.

Black Rainbow: Legends of the Incas and Myths of Ancient Peru, translated and edited by John Bierhorst (Farrar Straus Giroux, 1976).

The Incas by Cottie Burland (Silver, 1979).

Let's Visit Bolivia by John Griffiths (Burke, 1985).

Monuments of the Incas by John Hemming (New York Graphic Society, 1982).

The Conquest of the Incas by John Hemming (Macmillan, 1970).

We Live in Chile by Alex Huber (Watts, 1986).

Let's Visit Chile by Garry Lyle (Burke, 1984).

The Incredible Incas and their Timeless Land by Loren McIntyre (National Geographic Society, Washington, 1975).

The Incas by Anne Millard (Watts, 1980).

Atahuallpa and the Incas by Marion Morrison (Watts, 1986).

Glossary of Indian and Spanish Words

Aguayo Brightly colored shawl worn by Indian women.

Altiplano High mountain plain around Lake Titicaca.

Ayllu A social and organizational group of people, usually related by blood.

Barriadas The slums found around big towns.

Campesino Word meaning peasant, generally used in Bolivia instead of "Indian."

Cholo Word used in Bolivia for a "mestizo" or person of mixed Spanish and Indian blood.

Chullo Knitted hat worn by Indian men.

Chullpa Ancient Indian tomb or burial tower built above ground.

Coca Leaves from the coca bush that are chewed by the Indians.

Conquistador A Spanish soldier.

Cordillera A mountain chain.

Criollo Spaniards of pure blood born in the colonies.

Encomienda System by which Spanish landlords acquired an Indian work force, in return for teaching them the Christian faith.

Huaca A sacred place or thing.

Huaynos Popular songs for dancing.

Ichu Tough grass found in dry mountain regions.

Mestizo Person of mixed Spanish and Indian blood.

Mita Form of compulsory labor.

Peninsulares People born in Spain who settled in the colonies.

Polleras Colorful skirts worn by Aymara women.

Quinoa A nutritious cereal native to the Andes.

Quipu A string and knot device for recording numbers and some information.

Quipumayoc Keeper of a quipu.

Tambo A resting place used by the Incas on long journeys.

Acknowledgments

All the illustrations in this book, including the cover, were provided by Tony and Marion Morrison's South American Pictures, except for the following: Bill Donohoe, pages 6 and 12; Wayland Picture Library, pages 24 and 25 (both).

Index

Agriculture 7, 16, 23, 24, 25, 28, 30, 38, 40, 44
Aguayo 26
Alpaca 24
Altiplano 8, 36
Atahualpa (Inca Emperor) 14
Ayllus 12, 23
Aymara Indians 6, 19, 28, 30
  ancestors 8
  and revolts 19
  diet 23
  dress 26
  on Lake Titicaca 11
  religion 8, 20

Barriadas 43
Bolívar, Simón 19
Bolivia 6, 8, 16, 19, 26, 28, 30, 32, 34, 38, 42
Bolas 11

Campesino 28
Cerro Rico 16
Chaco War 28, 30
Chipaya Indians 10-11
Cholos 42
Chullo 26
Chullpa 10
Climate 23, 35
Coca 23, 34, 36-37, 38
  cocaine 37
Colombia 6
Colonizing lowlands 38
Columbus, Christopher 14
Conquistadores 16
Criollos 16
Cuzco 12, 20

Death 10, 16, 35
de San Martin, José 19
Disease 16, 18, 38
Dress 10, 25, 26, 40, 42

Ecuador 6, 12, 19, 28, 32, 38, 40, 41
Education 7, 28, 32, 45

Fiestas 20, 23, 25, 26
  Corpus Christi 20
  Inti Raimi 20
  Pachamama 20, 21, 37
  Thunupa 20
Food 11, 23

Guanaco 24
Gold 16

Hairstyles 10, 40
Health 28, 32, 34-35, 36, 45
Housing 10-11, 24, 43
Huaca 20
Hunting 11

Incas 6-7, 12-13, 44
  buildings 14
  craftsmen 14
  emperors 12, 14, 24
  extent of empire 12
  farming 12-13, 23
  festivals 20
  government 12, 13
  language 14
  mita 16
  storehouses 12
  Sun Temple 20
Independence struggle 7, 19, 44

Kallawaya Indians 34

Land reforms 28, 30, 45
La Paz 19, 42
Llama 10, 24-25

Machu Picchu 14
Mestizos 18, 30, 42-43, 45

Nationalization 28

Otavalo Indians 40-41

Pachacuti Inca 12
Paraguay 28
Peninsulares 18
Peru 6, 7, 12, 14, 19, 28, 32, 38, 42
Pizarro, Francisco 7, 14
Pollera 26, 42
Population 42
Potosi 16, 18

Quechua Indians 6, 19, 28, 30
  ancestors 8
  and revolts 19
  dress 26
  religion 8, 20

Religion 16, 19, 20-21
Revolts 18, 19

Spanish conquest 7, 14, 16, 18, 30, 42, 44
  and *encomienda* 16
  and religion 16
  and slavery 7, 16
  and taxes 16

Tambos 12
Textile industry 40-41
Titicaca, Lake 6, 8, 11, 23
Tiwanaku 8
Topa Inca 12
Transportation
  animal 25, 30
  railroads 26, 30
  road, 30, 38

Vicuna 24
Viracocha 8
Voting 32